Advent and Christmas Wisdom from PADRE PIO

Daily Scripture and Prayers Together With Saint Pio of Pietrelcina's Own Words

Compiled by Anthony F. Chiffolo

A Redemptorist Publication

To Rusty and Lisa

Published by **Redemptorist Publications**
A Registered Charity limited by guarantee.
Registered in England
3261721

Imprimi Potest: Thomas D. Picton, C.Ss.R.
Provincial, Denver Province, The Redemptorists

Compilation, Prayer, and Action Copyright 2005 by Anthony F. Chiffolo

First Printed September 2005

Acknowledgments of sources of quotations from Saint Pio are listed on pages 101 to 104.

Printed in the United States of America
09 08 07 06 05   5 4 3 2 1
First edition

Redemptorist
P U B L I C A T I O N S

Alphonsus House Chawton Hampshire GU34 3HQ
Telephone: 01420 88222   Fax: 01420 88805
rp@ShineOnline.net   www.ShineOnline.net

Contents

Introduction

~ v ~

PART I

Readings for Advent

~ 1 ~

PART II

Readings for the Christmas Season

~ 59 ~

PART III

A Format for Evening Prayer

~ 87 ~

Acknowledgments and Sources

~ 101 ~

Epigraph

What do you seek on earth if not God?

–LETTERS

As the holy feast of Christmas approaches I feel obliged in conscience not to let it pass without wishing you a Christmas full of those heavenly consolations which your heart desires. Although I have always prayed for you who have been and will continue to be the person I love very dearly, during these days I shall not fail to redouble my prayers to the heavenly Infant, that He may be pleased to keep you from all harm in this world, especially from the misfortune of losing the Child Jesus.

–LETTERS

Introduction

"WHAT DO YOU SEEK on earth if not God?" So wrote Saint Padre Pio to the Ventrella Sisters, among those for whom he served as spiritual advisor, and so he might ask us the same question today. Pio, in fact, spent his entire life seeking God, longing not just to be close to God but to be one with God. And for Pio, the first step toward God was a spiritual engagement with the story of the Nativity.

It's easy to see Padre Pio as a Lent and Easter saint, a saint whose entire life was like a prolonged Good Friday on the cross. After all, beginning in September 1918, he bore the painful stigmata in his hands, feet, and side for many years, until just before his death in 1968. Yet it may be more difficult to see him as an Advent and Christmas saint, as a saint who leaps for joy at the news of an unexpected pregnancy, at the angels' announcement that a baby is born, at the Magi's discovery of a child beneath a star. But leap for joy he did. To express the incredible gift he experienced on Christmas day in 1917, the Christmas before his stigmatization, he wrote to his own spiritual director, Padre Agostino, "I cannot describe to you…all that I felt in my heart on that most happy night. My heart seemed to overflow with a holy love for our God become man….I was surfeited with spiritual joy."

Pio knew with complete certainty that at all times his place was beside Jesus, whether it be Jesus the suffering servant or Jesus the innocent babe. Providing some pre-Advent counsel, he wrote to the Ventrellas, "[O]ne thing only is necessary, to be close to

Jesus…." This was his lifelong quest, and his premier advice to all of his spiritual children.

"Be close to Jesus." It is good counsel for all of us as we experience another Advent. Perhaps in God's presence we are shy and reticent, or nervous and talkative, or fearful and belligerent, or brave and boastful. Does it really matter what we say or feel, or if we say or feel anything? Pio's enduring message to us is that only one thing counts: that we find a way to be with Jesus.

Will this Advent be different? Life-changing? It can be, if we accept as intended for us the invitation Pio extended to his spiritual children: "I urge you to unite with me and draw near to Jesus…."

This Advent, let us join him as he hastens to the God-Child, heeding the angels and following the star, to experience God's nearness, where anything and everything are possible.

HOW TO USE THIS BOOK

Advent—that period of great anticipatory joy—is a time of preparation for the celebration of Jesus' arrival in Bethlehem as a helpless infant. In the Western liturgy, Advent begins four Sundays prior to December 25—the Sunday closest to November 30, which is the feast of Saint Andrew, Jesus' first disciple. The annual commemoration of Jesus' birth begins the Christmas cycle of the liturgical year—a cycle that runs from Christmas Eve to the Sunday after the feast of the Epiphany. In keeping with the unfolding of the message of the liturgical year, this book is designed to be used during the entire period from the First Sunday of Advent to the end of the Christmas cycle. The four weeks of Advent are often thought of as symbolizing the four different ways that Jesus comes into the world: (1) at his birth as a helpless infant at Bethlehem; (2) at his arrival in the hearts of believers; (3) at his death; and (4) at his arrival on Judgment Day.

Because Christmas falls on a different day of the week each year, the fourth week of Advent is never really finished; it is abruptly, joyously, and solemnly abrogated by the annual coming again of Jesus at Christmas. Christ's Second Coming will also one day abruptly interrupt our sojourn here on earth.

Since the calendar dictates the number of days in Advent, this book includes Scripture and meditation readings for a full twenty-eight days. These twenty-eight daily readings make up part I of this book. It is suggested that the reader begin at the beginning and, on Christmas, switch to part II, which contains materials for the twelve days of Christmas. If there are any "extra" entries from part I, these may be read by doubling up days, if so desired, or by reading two entries on weekends. Alternately, one may just skip these entries that do not fit within the Advent time frame for that particular year.

Part III of this book proposes two optional formats for using each daily entry as part of a longer liturgical observance similar to Night Prayer combined with a version of the Office of Readings. These options are for those who may wish to use this book as part of a more-developed individual or group observance. The purpose of these readings is to enrich the Advent/Christmas/Epiphany season of the liturgical year and set up a means by which individuals, families, or groups may observe the true meaning of the season.

PART I

~~~~~~

READINGS *for* ADVENT

DAY 1

Seeking the Infinite Good

I seem to be searching continually for something I cannot find, and even I myself do not know what I seek. I love and suffer very little and I wish I could love much more this thing I am seeking. I would like to suffer much more for the ideal I am pursuing.

But…although I don't know what this good is that my heart of its own accord seeks so avidly, I seem to know one thing for certain, that this good is inexhaustible and not circumscribed by limits. I seem to understand, moreover, that my heart will never be able to contain it entirely, for in my ignorance I feel that this is a very great good, an immense good, an infinite good.

Is this Jesus?

If not, then who is it? *—LETTERS*

And he said to them, "Suppose one of you has a friend, and you go to him at midnight and say to him, 'Friend, lend me three loaves of bread; for a friend of mine has arrived, and I have nothing to set before him.' And he answers from within, 'Do not bother me; the door has already been locked, and my children are with me in bed; I cannot get up and give you anything.' I tell you, even though he will not get up and give him anything because he is his friend, at least because of his persistence he will get up and give him whatever he needs.

"So I say to you, Ask, and it will be given you; search, and you will find; knock, and the door will be opened for you. For everyone who asks receives, and everyone who searches finds, and for everyone who knocks, the door will be opened. Is there anyone among you who, if your child asks for a fish, will give a snake instead of a fish? Or if the child asks for an egg, will give a scorpion? If you then, who are evil, know how to give good gifts to your children, how much more will the heavenly Father give the Holy Spirit to those who ask him!" –LUKE 11:5–13

PRAYER

Come to me, O Infinite Good, as I begin my Advent journey. Send me your Spirit, that I may have the desire to seek you, the courage to knock on the doorway that opens upon the road to Bethlehem, and the willingness to ask for what I need along the way. Amen.

ADVENT ACTION

I will spend twenty minutes today contemplating what, if anything, is missing from my life, and I will organize a plan of action for this Advent from what I discern are my needs.

BLESSING

Don't tire yourself trying to find outside yourself that which is within you. Jesus is with you; He is yours and nobody will take Him away from you. –LETTERS

DAY 2

Desiring to Love

I want to love Jesus as I should. I desire this love; I know I love Him, but—dear God!—how inferior my love is to my desire to love! Ought it not to be the opposite, that my love should surpass the desire for it? *–LETTERS*

And this is my prayer, that your love may overflow more and more with knowledge and full insight to help you to determine what is best, so that in the day of Christ you may be pure and blameless, having produced the harvest of righteousness that comes through Jesus Christ for the glory and praise of God. –PHILIPPIANS 1:9–11

PRAYER

My life is dry, analytic, detached—a wasteland. My desire to love consumes me, but I feel nothing—no love, no connection, no joy. O Love, ignite my passion. Move me beyond self-examination so that I might begin to live a lover's life, bearing your love to the beloved community and sharing in the love that animates all of creation. Amen.

ADVENT ACTION

Today I will list all those people, places, experiences, and things that I love. With whom or which do I feel the strongest connection? Who or which excites my greatest passions? What do these choices say about how I choose to love?

BLESSING

May the heavenly Child always be at the center of your heart; may He sustain it, enlighten it, inspire it and transform it to His eternal love!

This is the most ardent prayer I say for you in these days before the stable of Bethlehem. Oh how dearly I hope the divine Infant will grant you this prayer! May Jesus continue to grant His graces to all, especially to you, giving you courage and resignation up to the last day of your pilgrimage. —*LETTERS*

DAY 3

Saying Yes!

*L*isten: By saying "Yes," only "yes," *fiat secundum verbum tuum* ["let it be done according to your word"], in order to obey the will of God, Mary became the Mother of the Most High, declaring Herself to be His maidservant, but preserving Her virginity which was so dear to God and to Her.

Because of that "yes," uttered by Mary Most Holy, the world obtained salvation; humanity was redeemed.

Let us, too, always obey God's will, and always say "yes" to our Lord. –ARCHIVES

> *In the sixth month the angel Gabriel was sent by God to a town in Galilee called Nazareth, to a virgin engaged to a man whose name was Joseph, of the house of David. The virgin's name was Mary. And he came to her and said, "Greetings, favored one! The Lord is with you." But she was much perplexed by his words and pondered what sort of greeting this might be. The angel said to her, "Do not be*

afraid, Mary, for you have found favor with God. And now, you will conceive in your womb and bear a son, and you will name him Jesus...." Mary said to the angel, "How can this be, since I am a virgin?" The angel said to her, "The Holy Spirit will come upon you, and the power of the Most High will overshadow you; therefore the child to be born will be holy; he will be called Son of God.... For nothing will be impossible with God." Then Mary said, "Here am I, the servant of the Lord; let it be with me according to your word." Then the angel departed from her. –LUKE 1:26–38

PRAYER

"No" is always my first response. "I can't do it" comes out of my mouth automatically. "No way!" and "Are you kidding?" and "I don't think so!" follow in sequence. I hesitate, I cavil, I demur, I decline, I refuse—and I die. O God of *Yes!* inspire me with your positive energy, that I might say "Yes" instead of "No." Help me believe that "I can do this." Open my mind to the amazing idea that with your Spirit, anything and everything are possible. Amen.

ADVENT ACTION

I will keep track of my answers today. How many times do I say "No"? "Yes"? Is there any discernible pattern? What do my responses reveal about my priorities?

BLESSING

Let us pray to the Lord that He may never permit us to shut the ears of our heart to His voice that is speaking to us today....
–*LETTERS*

Bursting with God-News

I tremble once more as I write to you. But why do I tremble?
I find it almost impossible to explain the action of the Beloved. In the immensity of his strength, Infinite love has at last
overcome my hardheartedness, leaving me weak and powerless.

He keeps pouring Himself completely into the small vase of
this creature and I suffer an unspeakable martyrdom because of
my inability to bear the weight of this immense love. How can I
carry the Infinite in this little heart of mine? Because of the
exultation of possessing Him in me, I cannot refrain from saying
with the most holy Virgin: *My spirit rejoices in God my Savior.*
—LETTERS

> *In those days Mary set out and went with haste to a Judean
> town in the hill country, where she entered the house of
> Zechariah and greeted Elizabeth. When Elizabeth heard
> Mary's greeting, the child leaped in her womb. And Elizabeth was filled with the Holy Spirit and exclaimed with a*

loud cry, "Blessed are you among women, and blessed is the fruit of your womb. And why has this happened to me, that the mother of my Lord comes to me? For as soon as I heard the sound of your greeting, the child in my womb leaped for joy. And blessed is she who believed that there would be a fulfillment of what was spoken to her by the Lord."
And Mary said,

> *"My soul magnifies the Lord,*
> *and my spirit rejoices in God my Savior."*
—Luke 1:39–47

Prayer

O God of Good News, when you bless me with God-News, bless me also with the Spirit of Annunciation, that I might share your joy with the whole of creation. Amen.

Advent Action

Today I will remember to notice the good things that come my way, and I will share the news with someone else—a family member, a friend, a coworker, or even a stranger.

Blessing

Mother Mary, lead me to the grotto of Bethlehem, so that I may indulge in the contemplation of the great and sublime event that is about to take place in the silence of the greatest and most beautiful night that the world has ever seen. —"Time of Birth"

Soaring Like Eagles

*A*t present I have come to the point where I am almost lost in this deep obscurity. Not a glimmer of light, not a moment's respite. I feel my courage failing and the thought that I am going astray, the idea that I may be offending God fills me with terror and paralyzes my limbs. Soul and body are pressed down by an enormous weight.

I feel as if all my bones were being dislocated and at the same time crushed and ground. The thought of God is what still sustains my soul. The idea that he is everywhere present affords scant consolation to my soul which no longer enjoys the presence of the Beloved and feels the harshness and the burden of its own solitude. —*LETTERS*

> *Why do you say, O Jacob,*
> *and speak, O Israel,*
> *"My way is hidden from the Lord,*
> *and my right is disregarded by my God"?*

Have you not known? Have you not heard?
The LORD is the everlasting God,
the Creator of the ends of the earth.
He does not faint or grow weary;
his understanding is unsearchable.
He gives power to the faint,
and strengthens the powerless.
Even youths will faint and be weary,
and the young will fall exhausted;
but those who wait for the LORD shall renew their strength,
they shall mount up with wings like eagles,
they shall run and not be weary,
they shall walk and not faint. —ISAIAH 40:27–31

PRAYER

It seems that the moment I began to focus on the spiritual experience of Advent, Bethlehem became like a mirage shimmering across the desert, beckoning elusively, tantalizingly, then vanishing completely. O God of Soaring Eagles, raise me above this obscurity, that I might once again glimpse my destination, and discern the path that will lead me to you. Amen.

ADVENT ACTION

I will spend thirty minutes today to "recharge my batteries" through simple prayer, quiet meditation, or a long-awaited nap.

BLESSING

May Jesus continue to totally possess your heart and treat you as a chosen one. —*LETTERS*

Following Unknown Paths

*N*ow and again a most feeble light penetrates from above, just enough to reassure my poor soul that all is being directed by divine Providence and that through joy and tears the heavenly Father is leading me by inscrutable secret ways to the end He has in view. This is nothing else than the perfection of my soul and its union with God. But then, alas, a little later my poor soul is plunged into a more tragic desolation than before....

Hence it is...that the bitterness of the trial is sweetened by the balm of God's goodness and mercy. Praise be to God who can so marvelously alternate joy and tears so as to lead the soul by unknown paths to the attainment of perfection.... –*LETTERS*

> *"I came to bring fire to the earth, and how I wish it were already kindled!"* –*LUKE 12:49*

PRAYER

The bright lights of the season are now blazing away, calling me to buy, to wrap, to bake, to decorate, to sing, and to shop some more. They are colorful; they twinkle with promises of fun and pleasure; and they light a very attractive path. But it is not necessarily the way you, my God, would have mapped out for me. O God of Unknown Paths, direct my footsteps by the light of your Spirit, that I might find you along those less-traveled roads that you have prepared for my journey. Amen.

ADVENT ACTION

Let me consider today the path my life has taken. Where is it leading me? What challenges can I expect along the way, and how will I deal with them?

BLESSING

I'll pray to the divine Infant in a special way to enable you to grow more and more in charity and to enkindle in your spirit the light of heavenly hope. –*LETTERS*

DAY 7

Awaiting the Dawn

*B*lessed are the eyes which will see the dawn of this new day! In the midst of the trial which has begun and which will be harsher for ourselves in particular let us look beyond this deep night and fix our gaze on the day that is to dawn, which will be sufficient to console us in our most sweet Lord. –*LETTERS*

> *Since all these things are to be dissolved in this way, what sort of persons ought you to be in leading lives of holiness and godliness, waiting for and hastening the coming of the day of God, because of which the heavens will be set ablaze and dissolved, and the elements will melt with fire? But, in accordance with his promise, we wait for new heavens and a new earth, where righteousness is at home. Therefore, beloved, while you are waiting for these things, strive to be found by him at peace, without spot or blemish.*
> *–2 PETER 3:11–14*

PRAYER

As Advent passes, the hours of daylight dwindle away, and a mood of darkness invades my spirit. Thank you, O God of Dawn, for reminding me that another part of the world is experiencing the opposite—a shortening of nighttime and an increase in daytime— and that the sunrise always follows even the longest night. Amen.

ADVENT ACTION

When the sun sets today I will light a candle to demonstrate how light overcomes darkness, and to symbolize the Light of Christ that has come into the world.

BLESSING

May Mary fill your heart with the flowers and fragrance of ever-fresh virtues, and place Her maternal hand on your head. Always keep close to our Heavenly Mother, because She is the sea that must be crossed, in order to reach the shores of eternal splendor in the kingdom of Dawn. –ARCHIVES

DAY 8

Hearing the Beloved Voice

ut praise be to God, for in the midst of this deep night of the soul one thing alone is left to me: the voice of the one who guides me. I follow this alone and only in this do I experience at times a slight calm in the midst of so many storms.
—*LETTERS*

> *He said, "Go out and stand on the mountain before the LORD, for the LORD is about to pass by." Now there was a great wind, so strong that it was splitting mountains and breaking rocks in pieces before the LORD, but the LORD was not in the wind; and after the wind an earthquake, but the LORD was not in the earthquake; and after the earthquake a fire, but the LORD was not in the fire; and after the fire a sound of sheer silence.* —*1 KINGS 19:11–12*

PRAYER

Because you are God of All Creation, you are certainly God of Noise as well. So why do I plead to be led out of the raucousness that surrounds me? You are in the racket as well as in the silence, calling me, loving me, just as you have promised. O Beloved Voice, I pray that I might hear you in the noisiest moments of my life, in those moments when I am deaf to the delightful song of creation, as well as in those moments of absolute stillness. Please grant me the grace to hear what you are saying to me—and to understand what I must do with my life. Amen.

ADVENT ACTION

Today I will turn off the radio and television and listen to those other sounds in my life that are often drowned out by the usual din. What messages or meanings are awaiting me in these sounds or silences?

BLESSING

I wish you, from the dear Redeemer, the grace of steadfastness of purpose, and especially that of being silent and letting everything around you be silent, in order to hear the voice of the Beloved and establish a peaceful dialogue with Him. –*LETTERS*

DAY 9

Blowing Where the Spirit Wills

We are not all called to the same state and the Holy Spirit doesn't work in all souls in the same way. He "blows as He wills and where He wills." –LETTERS

> *Jesus answered, "Very truly, I tell you, no one can enter the kingdom of God without being born of water and Spirit. What is born of the flesh is flesh, and what is born of the Spirit is spirit. Do not be astonished that I said to you, 'You must be born from above.' The wind blows where it chooses, and you hear the sound of it, but you do not know where it comes from or where it goes. So it is with everyone who is born of the Spirit." –JOHN 3:5–8*

PRAYER

Rogue waves and unpredictable gusts batter my soul, and I am foundering. O Divine Spirit, please grant me a little calmer sailing, or at least a short rest in a protected harbor. I do wish to go where you will—I just need to catch my breath before I can sail with you again. Amen.

ADVENT ACTION

I will leave a block of time, perhaps an hour or so, unplanned today and allow the Spirit to direct my life during those moments. Does the prospect of unstructured time make me uncomfortable or will I be able to readily follow where the Spirit leads?

BLESSING

May the grace of the divine Spirit always shine in your heart; sustaining, comforting, and possessing it! –LETTERS

DAY 10

Risking All

*I*n moments of greater spiritual oppression, place yourself in the presence of God and pronounce your *Fiat* ["Let it be"]! I know that sometimes you will not have the strength to do this, but do not fear. It is essential that you know Jesus is pleased with your spiritual state. Note that I say "know" and not "that you convince yourself." It is sufficient for you to know that Jesus is pleased with you and that you are on the true path. —*LETTERS*

"For it is as if a man, going on a journey, summoned his slaves and entrusted his property to them; to one he gave five talents, to another two, to another one, to each according to his ability. After a long time the master of those slaves came and settled accounts with them. Then the one who had received the five talents came forward, bringing five more talents, saying, 'Master, you handed over to me five talents; see, I have made five more talents.' His master said to him, 'Well done, good and trustworthy slave; you have been trustworthy in a few things, I will put you in charge of many things….' And the one with the two

talents also came forward, saying, 'Master, you handed over to me two talents; see, I have made two more talents.' His master said to him, 'Well done, good and trustworthy slave; you have been trustworthy in a few things, I will put you in charge of many things....' Then the one who had received the one talent also came forward, saying, 'Master, I knew that you were a harsh man, reaping where you did not sow, and gathering where you did not scatter seed; so I was afraid, and I went and hid your talent in the ground. Here you have what is yours.' But his master replied, 'You wicked and lazy slave! You knew, did you, that I reap where I did not sow, and gather where I did not scatter? Then you ought to have invested my money with the bankers, and on my return I would have received what was my own with interest. So take the talent from him, and give it to the one with the ten talents. For to all those who have, more will be given, and they will have an abundance; but from those who have nothing, even what they have will be taken away." –MATTHEW 25:14–30

PRAYER

Today it feels as if Advent were just another test, another trial to determine if I'm good enough to approach the crib on Christmas. Who is ordering this test: God, family, friends, the world around me, myself? Maybe I should consider abandoning Advent practices and Christmas preparations, and make my way directly to the manger, immediately, to be with you now and forevermore. Amen.

ADVENT ACTION

Today I will dare to do something I've always wanted but never had the courage to do, placing the outcome in God's hands.

BLESSING

May Jesus continue to look upon you with eyes of divine pleasure and may He transform you more in Him! –*LETTERS*

** DAY 11

Focusing on the Eternal

*O*hat should we say if we were to behold a poor peasant almost stupefied as he continued to gaze at a swiftly-flowing river? Perhaps we should just begin to laugh at him and with good reason. Is it not folly to fix our gaze on something that is rapidly passing? This, then, is the state of a person who fixes his eyes on visible things. For what are these things in reality? Are they perhaps different from a swiftly-flowing river on whose waters we have no sooner laid eyes than they disappear from our sight, never to be seen again?...

As for ourselves who have been called, through the goodness of the Most High God, to reign with the divine Bridegroom, whose minds are enlightened by God's true light, let us fix our gaze constantly on the splendor of the heavenly Jerusalem. Let the consideration of all those good things to be possessed in that realm provide us with delightful food for our thoughts. *–LETTERS*

"Do not store up for yourselves treasures on earth, where moth and rust consume and where thieves break in and steal; but store up for yourselves treasures in heaven, where neither moth nor rust consumes and where thieves do not break in and steal. For where your treasure is, there your heart will be also." –MATTHEW 6:19–21

PRAYER

O God of the Eternal, you have made me a physical being in a physical world that delights my senses and makes my days on earth joyful and pleasing. Yet there are people all around me who interpret your Word as a demand to abhor your creation, deprive the human senses, and avoid all physical pleasures in order to focus entirely and exclusively on the spiritual life. Help me find my way to your way, that I might enjoy the miraculous world you have created without obsessing about it, and without losing sight of the beautiful eternity that will, with your blessing, be my final and permanent home. Amen.

ADVENT ACTION

I will spend twenty minutes reflecting upon what I truly believe about life after death. What hopes do I have for the afterlife? What does "heaven" mean to me?

BLESSING

[L]et us pray that He may enlighten us more and more as to the immensity of the eternal inheritance which has been reserved for us by the goodness of the heavenly Father. May our discernment of this mystery turn our hearts away from earthly goods and make us eager to arrive at our heavenly home. –LETTERS

~~~~~ **DAY 12** ~~~~~~~~~~~~~~~~~~~~~~~~~~~~~~~~~~~~~~~

Following My Blessed Mother

We must make every effort, like many elect souls, to follow invariably this Blessed Mother, to walk close to her since there is no other path leading to life except the path followed by our Mother. Let us not refuse to take this path, we who want to reach our journey's end. –*LETTERS*

> [F]or wisdom, the fashioner of all things, taught me.
> There is in her a spirit that is intelligent, holy,
> unique, manifold, subtle, mobile, clear, unpolluted,
> distinct, invulnerable, loving the good, keen,
> irresistible, beneficent, humane,
> steadfast, sure, free from anxiety,
> all-powerful, overseeing all, and penetrating....
> For wisdom is more mobile than any motion;
> ...she pervades and penetrates all things.
> For she is a breath of the power of God,
> and a pure emanation of the glory of the Almighty;

~~~~~ 24 ~~~~~~

therefore nothing defiled gains entrance into her.
For she is a reflection of eternal light,
a spotless mirror of the working of God,
and an image of his goodness.
—WISDOM OF SOLOMON 7:22–26

PRAYER

O Blessed Mother, I am in awe of your journey, but I cannot follow in your footsteps. They are yours, and I feel God calling me to create my own, unique path through Eternity. Yet as I stumble to find my own road, please teach me how I might be as courageous, strong, and wise as you were, that I might experience love and joy and peace throughout my journey. Amen.

ADVENT ACTION

As today I consider the Blessed Mother's role in the life of her son, I will also think about my own mother and the role she plays in my life. How can I express my appreciation and gratitude to my mother for the influence she has had on my life?

BLESSING

My most pure Mother, my soul so poor…cries out to your maternal heart. In your goodness deign, I beseech you, to pour out on me at least a little of the grace that flowed into you with such infinite profusion from the Heart of God. Strengthened and supported by this grace, may I succeed in better loving and serving Almighty God, Who filled your heart completely, and Who created the temple of your body from the moment of your Immaculate Conception. —MEDITATION PRAYER ON MARY IMMACULATE

DAY 13

Heeding My Good Shepherd

To be afraid of being lost in the arms of divine Goodness is more peculiar than the fear of a baby held tightly in the arms of its mother. —LETTERS

"I am the good shepherd. The good shepherd lays down his life for the sheep. The hired hand, who is not the shepherd and does not own the sheep, sees the wolf coming and leaves the sheep and runs away—and the wolf snatches them and scatters them. The hired hand runs away because a hired hand does not care for the sheep. I am the good shepherd. I know my own and my own know me, just as the Father knows me and I know the Father. And I lay down my life for the sheep. I have other sheep that do not belong to this fold. I must bring them also, and they will listen to my voice. So there will be one flock, one shepherd." —JOHN 10:11–16

PRAYER

It's not so much that I'm afraid of being lost as it is that I'm afraid I was never found in the first place. Gather me in, O Good Shepherd, as a mother or a father might gather a newborn into a warm embrace, that I might know the comfort of your loving voice and the security of your loving touch. O how I long to feel safely enveloped in the arms of your love! Amen.

ADVENT ACTION

Today I will list those people who have been my mentors, guides, advisors, teachers, or gurus—all those who have been shepherds to me, who have helped shape me into the person I am at this moment. How have I honored them by passing on their teachings to others?

BLESSING

May the most holy Virgin present to God my feeble yet persevering prayers and by her purity persuade the heart of the Eternal Father to look upon us always with fatherly goodness.

May it please this Blessed Mother to make us worthy of eternal life. –*LETTERS*

Seeing Face-to-Face

*Y*ou are afraid that your love for God is not true love, that you do not love God at all. Well, I urge you to be quite at peace on this point.

…[B]e quite sure that God is not found where there is no desire for His love. Now, if the soul longs for nothing else than to love its God…then don't worry and be quite sure that this soul possesses everything, that it possesses God himself….[I]f it seems to you that you always desire without ever arriving at the posses- sion of perfect love, all this means that your soul must never say it has enough, it means that we cannot and must not stop on the path to divine love and holy perfection. St. Augustine says very aptly: *Our heart is not at rest till it rests in the object of its love.*

Now, you know very well that perfect love will be acquired when we shall possess the object of this love. But the object of this love will only be possessed when we shall see Him as He is, not through a veil but face to face, as St. Paul says, when we shall know Him as we know ourselves…. –*LETTERS*

For we know only in part, and we prophesy only in part; but when the complete comes, the partial will come to an end. When I was a child, I spoke like a child, I thought like a child, I reasoned like a child; when I became an adult, I put an end to childish ways. For now we see in a mirror, dimly, but then we will see face to face. Now I know only in part; then I will know fully, even as I have been fully known.
—1 CORINTHIANS 13:9–12

PRAYER

O God of Clear Seeing, I have never really seen you, for I have been looking for you in the grandeur of cathedrals and the silence of cloisters, in the splendor of sunsets and the sweetness of strawberries. I have sought you everywhere and in everything except in the very beings made in your image, in the people all around me. Teach me to recognize you in everyone so that I might clearly see how all the wonderful and beautiful faces I know are reflections of your all-encompassing and glorious being. Amen.

ADVENT ACTION

I will spend fifteen minutes today pondering all the ways I experience God's love in my day-to-day existence. How does my life reflect the love God has showered upon me?

BLESSING

One thing alone is necessary: to be close to Him, and you are. How happy you must be to be close to Jesus, and to be held so tightly to Him! You need do no more than what you are already doing; love this divine Goodness and abandon yourself to His arms and Heart. —LETTERS

Looking Within

*D*on't make any effort to look for God outside yourself, because He is there within you; He is with you, in your weeping and in your seeking. *–LETTERS*

> *For David says concerning him,*
>> *"I saw the Lord always before me,*
>>> *for he is at my right hand so that I will not be shaken;*
>> *therefore my heart was glad, and my tongue rejoiced;*
>>> *moreover my flesh will live in hope."*
>> *–ACTS 2:25–26*

PRAYER

Whenever I dare to look inside myself, I have a difficult time seeing divinity. I see greed, pride, selfishness, lust. I see loneliness, sadness, worry, anxiety. I see anger and cruelty, even hatred. Rarely do I see love, or joy, or contentment. O God Within, are you really present in such a mix? Or has my own negative energy pushed away your divine energy? O that I might allow you to rewire my interior life and realign the forces in my soul! Amen.

ADVENT ACTION

Today I will focus on reverencing the divine Spirit within everyone I encounter. At the end of the day, I will assess my experiences. Did others relate to me differently than I expected? Did I relate to others differently? Could I live my entire life this way?

BLESSING

May Jesus and Mary always be in your heart, and may they make you grow, more and more, in the beautiful virtue of charity which is the bond of Christian perfection. Amen. –LETTERS

DAY 16

Praying Simply

*Y*ou, too, must learn to more greatly recognize and adore divine will in all the events of life. Often repeat the divine words of our dearest Master: *Fiat voluntas Dei sicut in coelo et in terra* ["God's will be done on earth as it is in heaven"]. Yes, let this beautiful exclamation always be in your heart and on your lips throughout all the events of your life. Say it in times of affliction; say it in times of temptation and during the trials to which Jesus wants to subject you. Say it again when you feel yourself submerged in the ocean of love for Jesus; it will be your anchor and salvation. Do not fear the enemy; he will not launch anything against the little ship of your spirit because Jesus is the helmsman and Mary is the star. –*LETTERS*

"When you are praying, do not heap up empty phrases as the Gentiles do; for they think that they will be heard because of their many words. Do not be like them, for your Father knows what you need before you ask him.

"Pray then in this way:
Our Father in heaven,
hallowed be your name.
Your kingdom come.
Your will be done,
on earth as it is in heaven.
Give us this day our daily bread.
And forgive us our debts,
as we also have forgiven our debtors.
And do not bring us to the time of trial,
but rescue us from the evil one."
—MATTHEW 6:7–13

PRAYER

Dear Jesus, I recognize myself in what you once said to your disciples. I complicate my conversations with you, using too many words, those I once learned by heart and now repeat by rote, and those that emerge directly and immediately yet perhaps incoherently from my heart. O God of Simple Prayer, please see through this flood of words what I need and mean to say: that the deepest desire of my heart is to be in communion with you in all things. Amen.

ADVENT ACTION

I will take fifteen minutes today to pray in a new way, that is, using a prayer form that I don't usually follow. Does this enhance my communication with God?

BLESSING

May Jesus always rest in your heart, and may He allow you to rest at His feet! —LETTERS

DAY 17

Having God-Strength

*C*ourage, then, and go ahead. God is with you and hell, the world and the flesh will one day, to their confusion, have to relinquish their weapons and admit once more that they are powerless against the soul that possesses and is possessed by God....

You must have boundless faith in the divine goodness, for the victory is absolutely certain. How could you think otherwise? Isn't our God more concerned about our salvation than we are ourselves? Isn't He stronger than hell itself? Who can ever resist and overcome the King of the heavens? What are the world, the devil, the flesh and all our enemies before the Lord? *–LETTERS*

Finally, be strong in the Lord and in the strength of his power. Put on the whole armor of God, so that you may be able to stand against the wiles of the devil. For our struggle is not against enemies of blood and flesh, but against the rulers, against the authorities, against the cosmic powers of this present darkness, against the spiritual forces of evil in the heavenly places. Therefore take up the whole armor of God, so that you may be able to withstand on that evil day, and having done everything, to stand firm. –EPHESIANS 6:10–13

PRAYER

I do not recognize my life in the words of saints Pio or Paul. They experienced their lives as a series of pitched battles between agents of evil and angels of good. I experience my life as an ongoing struggle for illumination and revelation. O God who is my strength, help me embrace the saints' choicest tools, that I might have the courage to pray hard and long for insight and guidance, and that I might have the peace of knowing that all will be well, for your support for me surpasses all my understanding. Amen.

ADVENT ACTION

Today I will spend thirty minutes or an hour helping a person I know who is in greater need than I am, whose struggles or pains are larger than my own. Can I put aside my own needs, forget about myself, and focus entirely on someone else for this short period? How do I view my own needs now after this experience?

BLESSING

May Jesus be your companion, support and guide at all times and in all things!

On the happy occasion of the holy Nativity of the Infant Jesus, may you be pleased to receive my good wishes for everlasting well-being and eternal spiritual bliss. –*LETTERS*

DAY 18

Watching for Signs

You are suffering and are right to complain. By all means complain and in a loud voice, but fear nothing. The victim of Love is impatient to possess it; it must cry out that it can take no more and that it is impossible to resist the treatment of the Beloved who wants her and leaves her, and leaves her while he wants her. *—LETTERS*

Therefore the Lord himself will give you a sign. Look, the young woman is with child and shall bear a son, and shall name him Immanuel.—ISAIAH 7:14

PRAYER

I rejoice because in just a few short days the Virgin's son will be born again in my heart. But I also grieve, for I know only too well that this long-promised child will quickly grow up to be a man of sorrows, and too soon the man will be tested, tormented, and killed—leaving me bereft. Which sign am I supposed to trust then, O God of Signs, the promise of joy or the portent of grief? Is this coming-and-going supposed to signify hope? Is this giving-and-taking supposed to comfort and delight? It does not, and I can bear no more. Enough of signs pointing to a sad future. Let me enjoy today's brief expectation of happiness. It is all my heart can embrace. Amen.

ADVENT ACTION

I will list all the blessings I receive over the course of the day, and before retiring to bed I will thank God for these gifts. Is the list longer or shorter than I expected? What do my expectations say about my relationship with God?

BLESSING

May the Infant about to be born fill your heart with superabundant grace and make it ever more worthy of Himself!…

We are close to the feasts of the holy Infant, for which I express the wish that the Babe of Bethlehem may strengthen your heart by the fire of divine love and adorn your soul with the choicest virtues. –*LETTERS*

DAY 19

Praying Confidently

So when you feel oppressed by temptation, the means to *oblige* God to come to your aid is through humility of spirit, contrition of heart and confident prayer. It is impossible for God to be displeased with this demonstration; impossible for Him not to come to our aid and give in. It is true that God's power triumphs over everything; but humble and suffering prayer triumphs over God Himself! It lowers His arm, extinguishes His lightning, disarms Him, overcomes Him, appeases Him and makes Him, I would almost say a friend and dependent. –*LETTERS*

> Yet even now, says the LORD,
> > return to me with all your heart,
> with fasting, with weeping, and with mourning;
> > rend your hearts and not your clothing.

Return to the LORD, your God,
 for he is gracious and merciful,
slow to anger, and abounding in steadfast love,
 and relents from punishing. –JOEL 2:12–13

PRAYER

Today's distractions are driving me to complete distraction. Children crying for undivided attention. Partners asking for something that can't wait until tomorrow. Friends calling to unload about the latest family crisis. Coworkers seeking feedback on an urgent project. Dogs barking for dinner. Plants pleading for water. Laundry to fold, dishes to wash, even snow to shovel! How can I possibly do it all—and have any energy and time to give to you? O God who attends to all needs, please hear my plea and grant me some relief—some quiet time to calm myself and recollect what's really important in my life.

In the midst of this frantic day, help me create an uninterrupted moment of prayer with you. Amen.

ADVENT ACTION

In addition to my usual prayer time, I will set aside an extra fifteen minutes of quiet time so that I can talk further with God about what's in my heart. Does the extra time unlock my emotions? Am I able to listen to God's responses?

BLESSING

May Jesus and Mary always be with you and comfort you with their vigilant grace! –LETTERS

DAY 20

Pursuing God's Way to Heaven

*P*ay no attention to the path of trial, but...keep your eyes constantly fixed on He who guides you to the heavenly Homeland. Why should the soul be despondent? Why should it worry whether it reaches the Homeland by way of the desert or through fields?! As long as God is with you always and that you constantly arrive at the possession of the true Promised Land, why should the poor soul be afflicted?!

Believe me, Jesus is with you, so what do you fear? Take heart and fear nothing....We must see and speak to God amidst the thunder and the hurricanes. We must see Him in the burning bush amidst the fire and thorns. And in order to do this we must go barefoot and entirely renounce our own will and affections. Therefore, submit yourself to His holy will and do not believe that you would serve Him better in a different state, because one only serves Him well when one serves Him as he wishes.

—*LETTERS*

O God, you are my God, I seek you, my soul thirsts for you;
my flesh faints for you,
> *as in a dry and weary land where there is no water.*
So I have looked upon you in the sanctuary,
> *beholding your power and glory.*
Because your steadfast love is better than life,
> *my lips will praise you.*
So I will bless you as long as I live;
> *I will lift up my hands*
> *and call on your name.* —PSALM 63:1–4

PRAYER

This Bethlehem pilgrimage is too difficult this year. It's been so cold, and there's been so much snow and wind and ice, I think I'll just hibernate by the fire and skip over to spring. I don't want to venture into the blizzard to get to the Nativity play or the candle-lighting or the carol-singing. Tell me, O God of the Way, why must I leave my sanctuary now? Why must I risk the hazards of the unknown road you've opened before me? Will I find the Holy Child more easily now than later, when I might finally be ready to leave my safe closet? I'm so worn out by the mere thought of what lies ahead that I can barely move. Help me, please, to take just one more step on the way to you. Amen.

ADVENT ACTION

Today I will engage family or friends to join me in a spontaneous, unplanned outing, letting the Spirit lead us where God wills. How does this help us appreciate the unexpected at Christmas?

BLESSING

May the grace of the Holy Spirit always guide your heart and transform it completely! —LETTERS

DAY 21

Giving Thanks Along the Way

*Y*ou ought to ask Our Lord for just one thing: to love Him. All the rest should be thanksgiving. –*LETTERS*

Rejoice always, pray without ceasing, give thanks in all circumstances; for this is the will of God in Christ Jesus for you. –1 THESSALONIANS 5:16–18

Devote yourself to prayer, keeping alert in it with thanksgiving. –COLOSSIANS 4:2

PRAYER

Thanks be to God for pulling me out of my closet and placing me on the path to the stable this year. Though the snow be knee-deep and the air frigid, the vistas are absolutely spectacular—and my heart soars in jubilation and anticipation! Remind me of this magnificent experience, O God of the Way, whenever I fear the road ahead and hesitate to place all my trust in you. Amen.

ADVENT ACTION

In my hurry to get from place to place today I will make myself pause to notice the beauty with which God has surrounded me. Can I make such observation a habit and continue to appreciate the wonders that decorate my life?

BLESSING

May the Infant Jesus be born again in your heart; may He establish his dwelling place there and render you always more worthy of His divine embraces! —*LETTERS*

DAY 22

Thirsting for Living Water

I understand very well that nobody can worthily love God, but when a person does all he can himself and trusts in the divine mercy, why should Jesus reject one who is seeking Him like this? Has He not commanded us to love God with all the strength we have? Well, then, if you have given and consecrated everything you have to God, why are you afraid? Isn't it a real waste of time to dwell on it…?

On the other hand, you are always asking Jesus to do what you are unable to do yourself. Say to Jesus, as St. Augustine invariably said: *Give what you command and command what you will.* Do you want great love from me, Jesus? I too desire this, just as a deer longs to reach a flowing stream, but as you see I have no more love to give! Give me some more and I'll offer it to you! Do not doubt that Jesus who is so good will accept your offer, so be at peace. *—Letters*

As a deer longs for flowing streams,
    so my soul longs for you, O God.
My soul thirsts for God,
    for the living God.
When shall I come and behold
    the face of God? —PSALM 42:1–2

PRAYER

This final week of Advent finds me exhausted, not joyful, for the emotions of this year have completely wrung me out. I feel like that thirsty deer panting for a refreshing draught after having run a marathon through the woods. O God of Living Water, pour your Living Spirit into my soul. Fill my heart with a desire for you, only you, that I might press forward to the place of your birth and, finally, drink in the presence of that Love you so profligately spilled forth for all of creation. Amen.

ADVENT ACTION

I may be worn out, but assuredly there is someone I know who is even more exhausted and in need of support. Today I will spend thirty minutes or an hour helping someone with a problem or task that they can't handle alone. How do I feel afterward? Has helping someone else lifted my spirits? What will I do with this renewed energy?

BLESSING

May divine grace superabound in your heart always, and adorn your soul with new jewels! —*LETTERS*

DAY 23

Straining to "See"

I keep my eyes fixed on the East, in the night which surrounds me, to discover that miraculous star which guided our forebears to the Grotto of Bethlehem. But I strain my eyes in vain to see that luminary rise in the heavens. The more I fix my gaze the dimmer my sight becomes; the greater my effort, the more ardent my search, the deeper the darkness which envelops me. I am alone by day and by night and no ray of light comes through to enlighten me. –*LETTERS*

Once Jesus was asked by the Pharisees when the kingdom of God was coming, and he answered, "The kingdom of God is not coming with things that can be observed; nor will they say, 'Look, here it is!' or 'There it is!' For, in fact, the kingdom of God is among you." –LUKE 17:20–21

PRAYER

They say there is no time left for further preparations. They say you have already arrived, though I did not mark your coming. They say you are here, though I have not noticed you in the midst of your people. They say you will be with me always, but when will I recognize you? O God of "Seeing," please open my eyes to your abiding presence so that I might at last stop waiting for some future "birth" and start right now living a new life in you. Amen.

ADVENT ACTION

Today I will list all those people who have brought the Spirit of Christmas to me at some time in my life. Have I ever thanked them for their blessings? If not, I will write or call them today to do so.

BLESSING

May the Infant Jesus bless you, comfort you, reward you for what you are bearing for love of Him, and make you holy! –*LETTERS*

Believing Against the Evidence

*G*od is not present where there is not a desire to love Him.
–LETTERS

[H]is disciples were again in the house, and Thomas was with them. Although the doors were shut, Jesus came and stood among them and said, "Peace be with you." Then he said to Thomas, "Put your finger here and see my hands. Reach out your hand and put it in my side. Do not doubt but believe." Thomas answered him, "My Lord and my God!" Jesus said to him, "Have you believed because you have seen me? Blessed are those who have not seen and yet have come to believe." –JOHN 20:26–29

PRAYER

For so long I have tried to prepare myself for your birth anew in my heart, but today I have such doubts: doubts about the meaning, the possibility, and even the necessity of your Incarnation; doubts about my love for you and my worthiness to receive you; doubts about whether the story of your birth really has any meaning for me anymore. O God of Believing, I want to believe in the truth of the Incarnation. I want to trust that my love for you is real. I want to know that miracles beyond my wildest dreams are daily occurrences in your beloved community. Please, take charge of my unbelief so that I might come to know within my deepest soul that anything and everything are possible with your Spirit. Amen.

ADVENT ACTION

I will spend fifteen minutes reflecting upon those "miracles" that I have experienced firsthand over the years. What do such events tell me about God's presence in my life?

BLESSING

For the coming feasts of the Infant Jesus my wish for you is that your heart may be His cradle adorned with flowers, in which He can rest without the slightest discomfort.... –*LETTERS*

Accepting God's Giving

*D*on't worry about tomorrow, think only of doing good today, and when tomorrow comes, it will be today and then it is time enough to think of it.

We must have great confidence in divine Providence in order to practice holy simplicity....[W]e must imitate the people of God when they were in the desert. These people were severely forbidden to gather more manna than they needed for one day...do not doubt...that God will provide for the next day, and all the days of our pilgrimage. *–LETTERS*

He said to his disciples, "Therefore I tell you, do not worry about your life, what you will eat, or about your body, what you will wear. For life is more than food, and the body more than clothing. Consider the ravens: they neither sow nor reap, they have neither storehouse nor barn, and yet God feeds them. Of how much more value are you than the birds! And can any of you by worrying add a single hour to your span of life? If then you are not able to do so small a

thing as that, why do you worry about the rest? Consider the lilies, how they grow: they neither toil nor spin; yet I tell you, even Solomon in all his glory was not clothed like one of these. But if God so clothes the grass of the field, which is alive today and tomorrow is thrown into the oven, how much more will he clothe you—you of little faith!"
–Luke 12:22–28

PRAYER

O God of Giving, let me pause for a moment to appreciate the blessings you have bestowed upon me today: a tender note from my beloved, a hug from my child, a greeting from a faraway friend, a few moments sitting in the warm sunshine, a warm blueberry muffin, a sloppy kiss from my dog. Thank you for these and all the wonders of your creation. Amen.

ADVENT ACTION

Saint Pio exhorted his spiritual children to "think only of doing good today." What does "doing good" mean to me? How can I "do good" this day?

BLESSING

May the Child Jesus fill your heart with His heavenly graces and the most exquisite charisms; may He bless you, comfort you and make you holy! –*LETTERS*

Sailing Toward God

I beg you...not to worry about your own soul. Jesus loves you all the time and when Jesus loves, what is there to fear? Be careful all the time not to let your occupations upset your spiritual life and cause you anxiety, and although you set out over the waves and against the wind of many perplexities, keep your gaze fixed upwards and say to Our Lord continually: "Dear God, I am rowing and sailing for you; be my pilot and my oarsman yourself." —*LETTERS*

> *"Since much time had been lost and sailing was now dangerous...Paul advised them, saying, "Sirs, I can see that the voyage will be with danger and much heavy loss...."*
>
> *...[But] God has granted safety to all those who are sailing...so keep up your courage, men, for I have faith in God.* —*ACTS 27:9–10, 24–25*

Prayer

Advent is nearly ended, but I have not yet glimpsed my final destination. While I look for the end of the voyage, I have to ask if there even is one, or if the way itself is the only heaven I will ever know. O God my Pilot, I place my faith in your navigation, for I am sailing under your direction. Help me trust that right now I am on course and exactly where I need to be. Amen.

Advent Action

Let me pause today to look back over the past few weeks and "chart" my Advent journey. Can I discern a pattern in my experiences? Have they brought me closer to God?

Blessing

May Jesus, the sun of eternal justice and infinite and immense beauty always shine in your soul, warming and inflaming it with His holy love and rendering it more and more worthy of Him!
—*Letters*

Abandoning Myself to God

*W*hen will the moment come when the fog will be dispelled in my soul? When will the sun rise within me? Am I to hope for it in this world? I no longer believe this can happen. *—LETTERS*

Alas, I see myself astray in the deep dark night through which I am passing. But praise be to God, who never abandons anyone who hopes and places his trust in Him! *—LETTERS*

> *"Have pity on me, have pity on me,*
> > *O you my friends,*
> > > *for the hand of God has touched me!*
> *Why do you, like God, pursue me,*
> > *never satisfied with my flesh?*
> *O that my words were written down!*
> > *O that they were inscribed in a book!*

O that with an iron pen and with lead
  they were engraved on a rock forever!
For I know that my Redeemer lives,
  and that at the last he will stand upon the earth;
and after my skin has been thus destroyed,
  then in my flesh I shall see God,
whom I shall see on my side,
  and my eyes shall behold, and not another.
My heart faints within me!" –JOB 19:21–27

PRAYER

Why leave me alone now? The God-Child must be so close at hand, but I have no star nor angels to guide me to the manger, where you await my coming as much as I await yours. O God of Hope, I will not despair! I abandon myself entirely to your Providence, knowing that your Spirit is ever with me and will bring me safely home. Amen.

ADVENT ACTION

I will make a list today of all those people who have ever advised me in times of trouble or doubt, and I will pray that God will satisfy the needs of each one of them.

BLESSING

May Jesus continue to possess your heart, as you will one day possess His in the heavenly Homeland. –*LETTERS*

Christmas Eve

YEARNING WITH CONFIDENCE

*Y*ou know well that perfect love is acquired when one possesses the object of this love, which is God himself. But God will not be possessed totally and perfectly except in the Homeland; not while we are in exile. Therefore, as the total possession of God is not granted to the soul in exile, neither can Love possess consummated love, as long as this soul is a pilgrim on earth. Therefore, if this is our state, why so much frenzied anxiety and useless dejection? Yearn and yearn always, but see that it is with greater confidence, and without any fear. –*LETTERS*

> *On that day it shall be said to Jerusalem:*
> *Do not fear, O Zion;*
> > *do not let your hands grow weak.*
> *The LORD, your God, is in your midst,*
> > *a warrior who gives victory;*

he will rejoice over you with gladness,
he will renew you in his love;
he will exult over you with loud singing
as on a day of festival.
I will remove disaster from you,
so that you will not bear reproach for it.
I will deal with all your oppressors at that time.
And I will save the lame
and gather the outcast,
and I will change their shame into praise
and renown in all the earth.
At that time I will bring you home,
at the time when I gather you;
for I will make you renowned and praised
among all the peoples of the earth,
when I restore your fortunes
before your eyes, says the LORD.
–ZEPHANIAH 3:16–20

PRAYER

This night bursts with miraculous potential, for the long-awaited Incarnation is upon me. Yet every night—indeed, every instant—is just as pregnant with Divinity. O God of My Yearning, teach me to embrace the miraculous potential of every moment, to rejoice that the Divine breaks forth into creation every second of every day. Amen.

ADVENT ACTION

Tonight I will call or write a family member or a friend to wish them the blessings of the season.

BLESSING

May the Infant Jesus come down into your heart tonight and fill it completely with His divine love. –*LETTERS*

PART II

READINGS *for the* CHRISTMAS SEASON

Christmas Day

O IMMANUAEL!

I feel I am drowned in the immense ocean of the love of my Beloved. I am being surfeited continually with it.... My small heart is incapable of containing this immense love. It is true that it is inside and outside me. But, dear God, when you pour yourself into the little vase of my being I suffer the agony of not being able to contain you. The inner walls of this heart feel as if they were about to burst and I am surprised that this has not happened already.

It is also true that when the whole of this love is unable to enter such a little vase, it flows over onto the outside. How can one contain the Infinite in oneself? *–LETTERS*

Praise the LORD!
Praise the LORD from the heavens;
    praise him in the heights!
Praise him, all his angels;
    praise him, all his host!
Praise him, sun and moon;
    praise him, all you shining stars!
Praise him, you highest heavens,
    and you waters above the heavens!
Let them praise the name of the LORD,
    for he commanded and they were created.
He established them forever and ever;
    he fixed their bounds, which cannot be passed.
Praise the LORD from the earth,
    you sea monsters and all deeps,
fire and hail, snow and frost,
    stormy wind fulfilling his command!
Mountains and all hills,
    fruit trees and all cedars!
Wild animals and all cattle,
    creeping things and flying birds!
Kings of the earth and all peoples,
    princes and all rulers of the earth!
Young men and women alike,
    old and young together!
Let them praise the name of the LORD,
    for his name alone is exalted;
    his glory is above earth and heaven.
He has raised up a horn for his people,
    praise for all his faithful,
    for the people of Israel who are close to him.
Praise the LORD! —PSALM 148

PRAYER

Welcome, O Divine Birth! Make home within my heart, O Emmanuel! O may you overshadow me this day and every day, that I might become truly one with your Spirit. Amen.

CHRISTMAS ACTION

Although today will be busy with celebration, I will spend at least fifteen minutes before bedtime to reflect upon all the emotions I will have experienced. Am I at all surprised by my own feelings?

BLESSING

Dear God! I cannot describe to you…all that I felt in my heart on that most happy night. My heart seemed to overflow with a holy love for our God become man….I was overwhelmed by spiritual joy.

    May the heavenly Child arouse in your heart also all the holy emotions He made me feel during the holy night when He was laid in the poor little crib. –*LETTERS*

DAY 2

O Baby of Bethlehem!

[O]ne thing only is necessary, to be close to Jesus....[Y]ou know well that at the birth of Our Lord, the shepherds heard the divine and angelic singing of the heavenly spirits. Scripture tells us this, but it does not say that the Virgin, his Mother and Saint Joseph, who were closest to the Infant, heard the voices of the angels or saw those miraculous splendors. On the contrary, instead of hearing the angels singing, they heard the Child crying, and saw by the light of a poor lamp, the eyes of this divine Infant all wet with tears and trembling with cold.

Now, I ask you, wouldn't you have chosen to be in that dark stable filled with the cries of the little Child, rather than beside yourselves with joy, with the shepherds at this sweet heavenly melody, and the beauty of this admirable splendor? Yes, undoubtedly, you too would have exclaimed with Saint Peter: *It is good that we are here.*

You are nowhere but close to the Infant Jesus, trembling with cold in the stable of Bethlehem....Therefore, I beg you to love the crib of the Child of Bethlehem;...stay close to him and be sure that Jesus is in the midst of your hearts more than you could believe or imagine. –*LETTERS*

In that region there were shepherds living in the fields, keeping watch over their flock by night. Then an angel of the Lord stood before them, and the glory of the Lord shone around them, and they were terrified. But the angel said to them, "Do not be afraid; for see—I am bringing you good news of great joy for all the people: to you is born this day in the city of David a Savior, who is the Messiah, the Lord. This will be a sign for you: you will find a child wrapped in bands of cloth and lying in a manger." And suddenly there was with the angel a multitude of the heavenly host, praising God and saying,

> *"Glory to God in the highest heaven,*
>   *and on earth peace among those whom he favors!"*

*When the angels had left them and gone into heaven, the shepherds said to one another, "Let us go now to Bethlehem and see this thing that has taken place, which the Lord has made known to us." So they went with haste and found Mary and Joseph, and the child lying in the manger. When they saw this, they made known what had been told them about this child; and all who heard it were amazed at what the shepherds told them. But Mary treasured all these words and pondered them in her heart. The shepherds returned, glorifying and praising God for all they had heard and seen, as it had been told them. –*LUKE 2:8–20*

PRAYER

Though experience teaches me that seeing is indeed believing, I pause today to wonder if there might perhaps be a more important lesson: that believing is seeing. If the shepherds had not believed the angel, they would never have seen the child in the manger. And if I never believe in the birth of God's miraculous love, will I ever experience a love that surpasses all my understanding? O Baby of Bethlehem, help me believe in Love's incarnation, that I might come to dwell always in Love's abiding presence. Amen.

CHRISTMAS ACTION

Today I will list all the desires of my heart that seem to me to be impossible dreams. Then I will choose one—just one—to decide to believe in, with my whole heart and soul. And I will make a note of it and post it where I will see it every morning, to remind myself that with God, all things are possible.

BLESSING

[M]ay the light that flooded the minds of the devout shepherds of Bethlehem enlighten your mind also and never abandon you if this is best for your spirit. —*LETTERS*

O Child of Rapture!

Only once did I feel in the deepest recesses of my spirit something so delicate that I do not know how to explain it to you. First of all, without seeing anything, my soul became aware of His presence and then, as I would describe it, He came so close to my soul that I felt His touch. To give you a feeble image of it, it was like what happens when your body feels the pressure of another body against it.

I don't know how to describe it otherwise. I merely confess that I was seized with the greatest fear in the beginning and that by degrees this fear became a heavenly rapture. It seemed to me that I was no longer in the state of a traveler and I cannot tell you whether or not at that moment I was still aware of being in this body of mine. Only God knows this and I am unable to tell you anything further to give you a better idea of this event. —*LETTERS*

It is necessary to boast; nothing is to be gained by it, but I will go on to visions and revelations of the Lord. I know a person in Christ who fourteen years ago was caught up to the third heaven—whether in the body or out of the body I do not know; God knows. And I know that such a person—whether in the body or out of the body I do not know; God knows—was caught up into Paradise and heard things that are not to be told, that no mortal is permitted to repeat. On behalf of such a one I will boast, but on my own behalf I will not boast, except of my weaknesses. –2 CORINTHIANS 12:1–5

PRAYER

If I abandon myself completely to God's Providence, will I lose myself entirely? Will I cease to exist? I hold on so tightly to my own precious identity that I just can't fully embrace the Divine. O Child of Rapture, ease my reservations, that I might learn from the experiences of the great mystics and take heart that with God, whatever happens, all will be well. Amen.

CHRISTMAS ACTION

I will "take inventory" today of everything I fear I truly cannot live without. What does this inventory say about my priorities? How can I begin to reprioritize my life?

BLESSING

[P]raise be to God in the highest heavens! He is my strength, He is the salvation of my soul, He is my portion forever. In Him I hope, in Him I trust and I will fear no evil. –LETTERS

DAY 4

O Child of Goodwill!

*L*ive joyfully and courageously…and don't extinguish the spirit of the Lord within you. I said, live joyfully and courageously, at least in the upper part of the spirit because the angel that foretold the birth of our little Lord, announces it happily and sings and proclaims joy, peace and happiness to men of goodwill so that there might be nobody who does not know that in order to receive this Child goodwill is sufficient. *—LETTERS*

> *Make a joyful noise to the LORD, all the earth.*
>   *Worship the LORD with gladness;*
>   *come into his presence with singing.*
> *Know that the LORD is God.*
>   *It is he that made us, and we are his;*
>   *we are his people, and the sheep of his pasture.*
> *Enter his gates with thanksgiving,*
>   *and his courts with praise.*
> *Give thanks to him, bless his name.*

For the LORD is good;
    his steadfast love endures forever,
    and his faithfulness to all generations. —PSALM 100

PRAYER

What is the meaning of *goodwill:* a will that is perfectly aligned with God's Spirit? If so, I am not ready to receive the holy Child. Any examination of my conscience reveals how often I fall short of God's will—in fact, I am usually uncertain about what the Divine desires of me. Yet I still desire to follow the Spirit. Is that enough? O Child of Goodwill, call me to yourself, for I desire to call upon you, that I might embrace the Love you embody and become more responsive to the divine promptings that you have placed within my heart. Amen.

CHRISTMAS ACTION

Today I will examine everything I feel "called" to do with my life. Have I followed my callings faithfully, willingly, or have I resisted?

BLESSING

I warmly bless you and wish you every blessing on the birth of the Babe of Bethlehem. *—LETTERS*

_ DAY 5 *_*

O New Creation!

*T*he bitterness of love is still sweet and its weight suave. There-fore, why do you continually say, when feeling its great trans-ports, that you are unable to contain it? Our heart is small, but it is expandable, and when it can no longer contain the grandeur of the Beloved, and resist its immense pressure, do not fear, because He is both inside and out; by pouring Himself into the interior, He will surround the walls. Like an open shell in the ocean, you will drink your fill and, exuberantly you will be surrounded and carried along by His power. *–LETTERS*

> *Then I saw a new heaven and a new earth; for the first heaven and the first earth had passed away, and the sea was no more. And I saw the holy city, the new Jerusalem, com-ing down out of heaven from God, prepared as a bride adorned for her husband. And I heard a loud voice from the throne saying,*

_ 70 *_*

"See, the home of God is among mortals.
He will dwell with them as their God;
they will be his peoples,
and God himself will be with them;
he will wipe every tear from their eyes.
Death will be no more;
mourning and crying and pain
will be no more,
for the first things have passed away."
And the one who was seated on the throne said, "See, I am
making all things new." –REVELATION 21:1–5

PRAYER

When you pour your Spirit over creation, the earth bursts forth in glorious splendor, in rainbow hues and dazzling rhapsodies. But when you shower me with your Spirit, do I break out in song or dance to praise your name? Do I look upon my neighbors with any increase of love? Do I even feel anything? O New Creation, create in me a more expansive heart, that I might absorb all the graces you bestow upon me and drink—oh so deeply!—my fill from your eternal spring of Love. Amen.

CHRISTMAS ACTION

At least once today I will sing a song or recite a poem or a psalm of adoration and praise to our Creator God. How can I find ways to praise God on a more regular basis?

BLESSING

May the Infant Jesus always reign in your heart; may He be born again in your heart, fill it with His divine charisms and transform it totally…. –*LETTERS*

O Baby of Simplicity!

*J*esus likes to give himself to simple souls; we must make an effort to acquire this beautiful virtue of simplicity and to hold it in great esteem. Jesus said: *Unless you turn and become like children, you will never enter the kingdom of heaven.* But before He taught us this by His words he had already put it into practice. He became a child and gave us the example of that simplicity He was to teach us later also by His words. –*LETTERS*

> *People were bringing little children to him in order that he might touch them; and the disciples spoke sternly to them. But when Jesus saw this, he was indignant and said to them, "Let the little children come to me; do not stop them; for it is to such as these that the kingdom of God belongs. Truly I tell you, whoever does not receive the kingdom of God as a little child will never enter it." And he took them up in his arms, laid his hands on them, and blessed them.*
> *– MARK 10:13–16*

PRAYER

The message of Christmas is so simple: God became a human child, to show us how to live as human beings. What could be more straightforward? Yet I insist on questioning. How could God step out of God-time and into our-time? How could the child be both human and divine? How can the example of a life lived by a deity be the pattern for my own life? O Baby of Simplicity, as you lay in the manger, neither Mary nor Joseph pondered such conundrums. All they thought of was your needing them, and they gave you food and shelter and comfort. Help me learn from their example, that I might put philosophy aside and focus my attention on the children of God who are right in front of me, to attend to their immediate needs. Amen.

CHRISTMAS ACTION

I will spend a half hour or so visiting with someone who is lonely and in need of friendship and love. How might I make this a regular habit?

BLESSING

May the heavenly Child always be at the center of your heart; may He govern it, enlighten it, vivify it and transform it to His eternal love! –*LETTERS*

O Child Given for Me!

*J*urge you to unite with me and draw near to Jesus with me to receive His embrace and a kiss that sanctifies and saves us. For this purpose let us listen to the holy king David who invites us to kiss the Son devoutly: *Deal gently with the son,* for this son of whom the royal prophet speaks is none other than the one of whom the prophet Isaiah said: *For to us a child is born, to us a son is given.* –LETTERS

> For a child has been born for us,
>   a son given to us;
> authority rests upon his shoulders;
>   and he is named
> Wonderful Counselor, Mighty God,
>   Everlasting Father, Prince of Peace.
> His authority shall grow continually,
>   and there shall be endless peace
> for the throne of David and his kingdom.

He will establish and uphold it
with justice and with righteousness
from this time onward and forevermore.
The zeal of the LORD *of hosts will do this. —*ISAIAH 9:6–7

PRAYER

The children all around me rejoice at Christmastime, for their joy is complete: they have new toys and plenty of free days to play and enjoy themselves with total abandon. Are the children hidden deeply within the adults so joyful at your coming? Or feeling at all blessed or happy? O Child Given for Me, touch my heart with your newly born wonder, that I might remember how I once experienced this season. I desire to savor all the moments of my life with awe, joy, and love—your simple yet precious gifts to all children. Amen.

CHRISTMAS ACTION

I will allow myself to play for at least a half hour today: at cards, checkers, charades, or any game that is simply fun for its own sake. Can I find a way to incorporate play more frequently into my life?

BLESSING

May the joy of the divine Spirit always fill your heart, and those of all souls who want to be faithful to His holy grace! —*LETTERS*

O Infant of the Manger!

*O*h Christians, how varied and numerous are the teachings that depart from the grotto of Bethlehem! Oh, how the heart should burn with love for Him who very affectionately became man for us. We should have a burning desire to lead the world to this humble grotto, refuge of the King of Kings, greater than any royal palace of human beings, because it was God's home and throne! Let us ask the Divine Child to clothe us with humility because only by this virtue can we enjoy this mystery which is so full of divine affection. —"Time of Birth"

Joseph also went from the town of Nazareth in Galilee to Judea, to the city of David called Bethlehem, because he was descended from the house and family of David. He went to be registered with Mary, to whom he was engaged and who was expecting a child. While they were there, the time came for her to deliver her child. And she gave birth to her firstborn son and wrapped him in bands of cloth, and laid him in a manger, because there was no place for them in the inn –LUKE 2:4–7

PRAYER

What was that manger but an animal's feeding trough, that grotto but a smelly barn for goats and donkeys? Unfit for human habitation? Yet how many people today do not have even that much shelter or comfort? O Infant of the Manger, remind me of the desperation still rampant among your people, and create in me a reckless spirit of giving, that I might begin immediately to share the abundance my loving God has provided me with those whose needs are so much greater than my own. Amen.

CHRISTMAS ACTION

I will do something for the homeless or less fortunate people in my community today, helping clean up at the shelter, serving food at the soup kitchen, bringing some hats and mittens or a coat to someone who does not have warm winter clothing. How can I make this kind of service more than a seasonal consideration?

BLESSING

May the divine Infant whose birth we are celebrating in these days totally possess your heart, and transform it more and more to His! –*LETTERS*

DAY 9

O Child of Humility!

Stay very close to the crib of this gentle Child, especially during these holy days of his birth. If you love wealth, here you will find the gold the Magi left Him; if you love the smoke of honor, you will find that of the incense; and if you love the delicacy of the senses, you will smell the perfumed myrrh which perfumes the entire holy stable. Have a great love for this heavenly Infant. Be respectful in the familiarity you will gain with Him through prayer, and joyful when you feel within you holy inspirations and the desire to be especially His. *–LETTERS*

Let the same mind be in you that was in Christ Jesus,
who, though he was in the form of God,
did not regard equality with God
as something to be exploited,
but emptied himself,
taking the form of a slave,
being born in human likeness.

And being found in human form,
he humbled himself
and became obedient to the point of death....
—PHILIPPIANS 2:5–7

PRAYER

What happened to those rich gifts bestowed by the Magi? Was there enough myrrh to mask the odor in the cave where you were born? Enough gold to sustain your family during your Egyptian exile? Enough incense to accompany your mother and father's prayers for your safety? O Child of Humility, you required no royal gifts and kept nothing for yourself, not even your very life. Do you need anything from me? All I can offer is to be with you, to pray with you, and to share my love with you. I return now in spirit to the grotto of Bethlehem, to wait upon my God. Amen.

CHRISTMAS ACTION

Today I will take inventory of my extravagances and excesses. Is there a way for me to convert some of my extras into something really needed by people less fortunate than I?

BLESSINGS

May the Infant Jesus, reborn in your heart, always reign there; may He transform your heart totally, and fill it with His divine spirit! —LETTERS

O God Who Beckons!

*B*y means of the angels, Jesus calls the poor and simple shepherds in order to manifest Himself to them. He calls the learned men by means of their science. And all of them, moved by His inner grace, hasten to adore Him. He calls all of us by divine inspiration, and communicates with us by means of His grace. How many times has He invited us, too? And how readily have we responded? My God, I blush and become embarrassed when I have to answer such a question. –"TIME OF BIRTH"

Jesus said to him, "If you wish to be perfect, go, sell your possessions, and give the money to the poor, and you will have treasure in heaven; then come, follow me." When the young man heard this word, he went away grieving, for he had many possessions.

Then Jesus said to his disciples, "Truly I tell you, it will be hard for a rich person to enter the kingdom of heaven. Again I tell you, it is easier for a camel to go through the eye

of a needle than for someone who is rich to enter the king-
dom of God....Truly I tell you, at the renewal of all things,
when the Son of Man is seated on the throne of his glory,
you who have followed me will also sit on twelve thrones,
judging the twelve tribes of Israel. And everyone who has
left houses or brothers or sisters or father or mother or chil-
dren or fields, for my name's sake, will receive a hundred-
fold, and will inherit eternal life." –MATTHEW 19:21–29

PRAYER

When I was younger and my hearing better, I knew your voice
resounding in the depths of my soul, and I rejoiced that you took
notice of me. But I never responded, never followed, and your
glorious voice faded away, replaced sometimes by a cacophony
or, worse, silence. O God Who Beckons, I long to hear you once
more, to know that you have not forsaken me. Please call me again,
and yet again, that I might be welcomed into your everlasting
presence, the home that I have been seeking all my days. Amen.

CHRISTMAS ACTION

I will go to the library or bookstore and take home a book about
someone whose life followed an unusual path because of an ex-
traordinary call from God. As I read about this person, I will consider how I might cope if God were to suddenly turn my world
upside down.

BLESSINGS

May the divine Child accomplish the transformation of your
heart, fulfilling in you and for you, His holy will. *–LETTERS*

O Child, Word of God!

When Mass was over I remained with Jesus in thanksgiving. Oh, how sweet was the colloquy with paradise that morning!…The heart of Jesus and my own—allow me to use the expression—were fused. No longer were two hearts beating but only one. My own heart had disappeared, as a drop of water is lost in the ocean. Jesus was its paradise, its king. My joy was so intense and deep that I could bear no more and tears of happiness poured down my cheeks. –*LETTERS*

And the Word became flesh and lived among us, and we have seen his glory, the glory as of a father's only son, full of grace and truth. (John testified to him and cried out, "This was he of whom I said, 'He who comes after me ranks ahead of me because he was before me.'") From his fullness we have all received, grace upon grace. The law indeed was given through Moses; grace and truth came through Jesus Christ. No one has ever seen God. It is God the only Son, who is close to the Father's heart, who has made him known. –JOHN 1:14–18

PRAYER

Each day is a new revelation, each moment a new incarnation, a renewed infusion of the Divine as God pours and pours the Word into this wild pool of creation. O Child, Word of God, do any ripples reach my soul? Sensitize my heart to your abiding presence, that I might recognize the ongoing incarnation of the Word in my life, rejoice at all God-expressions, and share these extravagant blessings with all of God's people. Amen.

CHRISTMAS ACTION

I will share a word of kindness or love with each person I encounter throughout the day. How does this activity change the way I feel about other people and the way they might feel about me?

BLESSINGS

May Jesus always be the supreme King of your heart; may He grant the ardent prayers which He Himself places in your heart, and truly fill it with His holy and divine love! Amen. –*LETTERS*

DAY 12

O Star-Blessed Child!

*G*ive me, and preserve in me, that ardent faith which will make me believe and work for Your love alone. My first gift to You, together with the Holy Magi, prostrated at Your feet, will be to declare, without any human regard for the entire world, that You are our one and only true God. –"Time of Birth"

In the time of King Herod, after Jesus was born in Bethlehem of Judea, wise men from the East came to Jerusalem, asking, "Where is the child who has been born king of the Jews? For we observed his star at its rising, and have come to pay him homage." When King Herod heard this, he was frightened, and all Jerusalem with him; and calling together all the chief priests and scribes of the people, he inquired of them where the Messiah was to be born. They told him, "In Bethlehem of Judea; for so it has been written by the prophet: / 'And you, Bethlehem, in the land of Judah, / are by no means least among the rulers of Judah; / for from you shall come a ruler / who is to shepherd my people Israel.'" / Then Herod secretly called for the wise men and learned from them the exact time when the star had appeared. Then he sent them to Bethlehem, saying, "Go and search diligently for the child; and when you have found him, bring me word so that I may also go and pay him homage." When they had heard the king, they set out; and there, ahead of them, went the star that they had seen at its rising, until it stopped over the place where the child was. When they saw that the star had stopped, they were overwhelmed with joy. On entering the house, they saw the child with Mary his mother; and they knelt down and paid him homage. Then, opening their treasure chests, they offered him gifts of gold, frankincense, and myrrh. –MATTHEW 2:1–11

PRAYER

I commit myself to follow your star, O Star-Blessed Child, both today and throughout the coming year. As the shepherds and the Magi bore the good news of your coming to the wider world, so may I also be anointed as a messenger, to bear the good news of your living presence to all of creation. Amen.

CHRISTMAS ACTION

Today I will share my life story with a colleague, a friend, or a family member, and I will ask him or her to do the same. How does this help bring us to a closer relationship?

BLESSINGS

May Jesus be the star which guides our steps constantly in the wilderness of this present life and bring us without delay to the haven of salvation! –*LETTERS*

Final Blessings

[T]his life is short, the rewards for what we achieve in it are eternal. Let us do good, adhere to the will of God; let this be the star on which we rest our gaze during this navigation, because in this way we cannot but reach the heavenly port. Let us not silence our expectations of the holy eternity to which we aspire. —*LETTERS*

The palm of glory is reserved only for those who fight valiantly till the end. Therefore, let us begin our holy battle this year. God will help us and crown us with eternal triumph. —"TIME OF BIRTH"

May the grace of the divine Spirit always dwell in your heart until it is completely transformed into God! Always, every day, not to say at every moment I remember you before our most sweet Lord and He alone knows what ardent prayers I offer for you. May it please this dear Redeemer to grant them all. —*LETTERS*

PART III

~~~~~~

A Format for Evening Prayer

Format for Nightly Prayer and Reading

THE PURPOSE OF PRESENTING these two optional formats for nightly readings and prayer is to offer different ways to use the material in this book for group or individual prayer. Of course, there are other ways in which to use this book—for example, as a meditative daily reader or as a guide for a prayer journal—but the following familiar liturgical formats provide a structure that can be used in a variety of contexts.

FORMAT 1

OPENING PRAYER

The observance begins with these words:

God, come to my assistance.
Lord, make haste to help me.

followed by:

Glory to the Father, and to the Son,
and to the Holy Spirit, as it was in the beginning,
is now, and will be, for ever. Amen. Alleluia!

EXAMINATION OF CONSCIENCE

If this observance is being prayed individually, an examination of conscience may be included. Here is a short examination of conscience; you may, of course, use your own preferred method.

1. Place yourself in a quiet frame of mind.
2. Review your life since your last confession.
3. Reflect on the Ten Commandments and any sins against these commandments.
4. Reflect on the words of the gospel, especially Jesus' commandment to love your neighbor as yourself.
5. Ask yourself these questions: How have I been unkind in thoughts, words, and actions? Am I refusing to forgive anyone? Do I despise any group or person? Am I a prisoner of fear, anxiety, worry, guilt, inferiority, or hatred of myself?

PENITENTIAL RITE (OPTIONAL)

If a group of people are praying in unison, a penitential rite from the Roman Missal may be used:

Presider: Lord Jesus, you came to call all people to yourself:
Lord, have mercy.

All: Lord, have mercy.

Presider: Lord Jesus, you come to us in word and prayer:
Christ, have mercy.

All: Christ, have mercy.

Presider: Lord Jesus, you will appear in glory with all your saints:
Lord, have mercy.

All: Lord, have mercy.

Presider: May almighty God have mercy on us, forgive us our sins, and bring us to life everlasting.

All: Amen.

Hymn: "O Come, O Come, Emmanuel"

A hymn is now sung or recited. This Advent hymn is a paraphrase of the great "O" Antiphons written in the twelfth century and translated by John Mason Neale in 1852.

O come, O come, Emmanuel,
And ransom captive Israel;
That mourns in lonely exile here,
Until the Son of God appear.

Refrain: Rejoice! Rejoice!
　　　　 O Israel! To thee shall come, Emmanuel!

O come, thou wisdom, from on high,
And order all things far and nigh;
To us the path of knowledge show,
And teach us in her ways to go.

Refrain

O come, O come, thou Lord of might,
Who to thy tribes on Sinai's height
In ancient times did give the law,
In cloud, and majesty, and awe.

Refrain

O come, thou rod of Jesse's stem,
From ev'ry foe deliver them
That trust thy mighty power to save,
And give them vict'ry o'er the grave.

Refrain

O come, thou key of David, come,
And open wide our heav'nly home,
Make safe the way that leads on high,
That we no more have cause to sigh.

Refrain

O come, thou Dayspring from on high,
And cheer us by thy drawing nigh;
Disperse the gloomy clouds of night
And death's dark shadow put to flight.

Refrain

O come, Desire of nations, bind
In one the hearts of all mankind;
Bid every strife and quarrel cease
And fill the world with heaven's peace.

Refrain

PSALM 27:7–14—GOD STANDS BY US IN DANGERS

Hear, O LORD, when I cry aloud,
    be gracious to me and answer me!
"Come," my heart says, "seek his face!"
    Your face, LORD, do I seek.
    Do not hide your face from me.

Do not turn your servant away in anger,
    you who have been my help.
Do not cast me off, do not forsake me,
    O God of my salvation!
If my father and mother forsake me,
    the LORD will take me up.

Teach me your way, O LORD,
>and lead me on a level path
>because of my enemies.
Do not give me up to the will of my adversaries,
>for false witnesses have risen against me,
>and they are breathing out violence.

I believe that I shall see the goodness of the LORD
>in the land of the living.
Wait for the LORD;
>be strong, and let your heart take courage;
>wait for the LORD!

RESPONSE

I long to see your face, O Lord. You are my light and my help. Do not turn away from me.

SCRIPTURE READING

Read silently or have a presider proclaim the Scripture of the day that is selected.

RESPONSE

Come and set us free, Lord God of power and might. Let your face shine on us and we will be saved.

>*Glory to the Father, and to the Son,*
>*and to the Holy Spirit, as it was in the beginning,*
>*is now, and will be for ever. Amen.*

SECOND READING

Read the excerpt from Saint Pio for the day selected.

CANTICLE OF SIMEON

Lord, now you let your servant go in peace;
  your word has been fulfilled:
My own eyes have seen the salvation
  which you have prepared in the sight of every people:
A light to reveal you to the nations
  and the glory of your people Israel.
Glory to the Father, and to the Son, and to the Holy Spirit,
as it was in the beginning, is now, and will be for ever. Amen.

PRAYER

Say the prayer that follows the selected excerpt from Saint Pio.

BLESSING

May the Lord grant us a restful night and a peaceful death. Amen.

MARIAN ANTIPHON

Loving mother of the Redeemer,
  gate of heaven, star of the sea,
  assist your people who have fallen yet strive to rise again.
To the wonderment of nature you bore your Creator,
  yet remained a virgin after as before.
You who received Gabriel's joyful greeting,
  have pity on us poor sinners.

FORMAT 2

OPENING PRAYER

The observance begins with these words:

God, come to my assistance.
Lord, make haste to help me.

followed by:

Glory to the Father, and to the Son,
and to the Holy Spirit, as it was in the beginning,
is now, and will be, for ever. Amen. Alleluia!

EXAMINATION OF CONSCIENCE

If this observance is being prayed individually, an examination of conscience may be included. Here is a short examination of conscience; you may, of course, use your own preferred method.

1. Place yourself in a quiet frame of mind.
2. Review your life since your last confession.
3. Reflect on the Ten Commandments and any sins against these commandments.
4. Reflect on the words of the gospel, especially Jesus' commandment to love your neighbor as yourself.
5. Ask yourself these questions: How have I been unkind in thoughts, words, and actions? Am I refusing to forgive anyone? Do I despise any group or person? Am I a prisoner of fear, anxiety, worry, guilt, inferiority, or hatred of myself?

PENITENTIAL RITE (OPTIONAL)

If a group of people are praying in unison, a penitential rite from the Roman Missal may be used:

All: I confess to almighty God,
           and to you, my brothers and sisters,
           that I have sinned through my own fault
           in my thoughts and in my words,
           in what I have done,
           and in what I have failed to do;
           and I ask blessed Mary, ever virgin,
           all the angels and saints,
           and you, my brothers and sisters,
           to pray for me to the Lord our God.
Presider: May almighty God have mercy on us,
           forgive us our sins,
           and bring us to life everlasting.
All: Amen.

Hymn: "Behold, a Rose"

A hymn is now sung or recited. This traditional hymn was composed in German in the fifteenth century. It is sung to the melody of the familiar "Lo, How a Rose E're Blooming."

Behold, a rose of Judah
From tender branch has sprung,
From Jesse's lineage coming,
As men of old have sung.
It came a flower bright
Amid the cold of winter,
When half spent was the night.

Isaiah has foretold it
In words of promise sure,
And Mary's arms enfold it,
A virgin meek and pure.
Through God's eternal will
She bore for men a savior
At midnight calm and still.

Psalm 40:1–8—Thanksgiving for Deliverance

I waited patiently for the LORD;
 he inclined to me and heard my cry.
He drew me up from the desolate pit,
 out of the miry bog,
and set my feet upon a rock,
 making my steps secure.
He put a new song in my mouth,
 a song of praise to our God.
Many will see and fear,
 and put their trust in the LORD.

Happy are those who make
   the LORD their trust,
who do not turn to the proud,
   to those who go astray after false gods.
You have multiplied, O LORD, my God,
   your wondrous deeds and your thoughts toward us;
   none can compare with you.
Were I to proclaim and tell of them,
   they would be more than can be counted.

Sacrifice and offering you do not desire,
   but you have given me an open ear.
Burnt offering and sin offering
   you have not required.
Then I said, "Here I am;
   in the scroll of the book it is
      written of me.
I delight to do your will, O my God;
   your law is within my heart."

RESPONSE

May all who seek after you be glad in the LORD, may those who find your salvation say with continuous praise, "Great is the LORD!"

SCRIPTURE READING

Read silently or have a presider proclaim the Scripture of the day that is selected.

RESPONSE

Lord, you who were made obedient unto death, teach us to always do the Father's will, so that, sanctified by the holy obedience that joins us to your sacrifice, we can count on your immense love in times of sorrow.

> *Glory to the Father, and to the Son,*
> *and to the Holy Spirit, as it was in the beginning,*
> *is now, and will be, for ever. Amen.*

SECOND READING

Read silently or have a presider read the words of Saint Pio for the day selected.

CANTICLE OF SIMEON

Lord, now you let your servant go in peace;
    your word has been fulfilled:
My own eyes have seen the salvation
    which you have prepared in the sight of every people:
A light to reveal you to the nations
    and the glory of your people Israel.
Glory to the Father, and to the Son, and to the Holy Spirit,
as it was in the beginning, is now, and will be for ever. Amen.

PRAYER

Recite the prayer that follows the excerpt from Saint Pio for the day selected.

BLESSING

Lord, give our bodies restful sleep and let the work we have done today bear fruit in eternal life. Watch over us as we rest in your peace. Amen.

MARIAN ANTIPHON

Hail, holy Queen, mother of mercy,
    our life, our sweetness, and our hope.
To you do we cry,
    poor banished children of Eve.
To you do we send up our sighs,
    mourning and weeping in this vale of tears.
Turn then, most gracious advocate,
    your eyes of mercy toward us,
    and after this exile
    show to us the blessed fruit of your womb, Jesus.
O clement, O loving,
O sweet Virgin Mary. Amen.

Acknowledgments and Sources

I THANK DANNY MICHAELS and his colleagues at Liguori Publications for their loving care in helping to bring this work to fruition. My special thanks go to (The Rev.) Dr. Rayner W. Hesse, Jr., for his invaluable assistance and, most of all, his hearty support of all that I am.

The following passages from Padre Pio's letters are reprinted from *Padre Pio of Pietrelcina Letters*, volume 1: Correspondence with his spiritual directors, 1910–1922. Ed. by Melchiorre of Pobladura and Alessandro of Ripabottoni, English version ed. by Gerardo Di Flumeri, O.F.M. Cap. San Giovanni Rotondo, Italy: Our Lady of Grace Capuchin Friary, 1984: second epigraph (to Padre Benedetto, Dec. 20, 1910), Advent 1 (to Padre Agostino, May 6, 1913), Advent 2 (to P. Benedetto, Apr. 7, 1915), Advent 4 (to P. Benedetto, Jan. 12, 1919), Advent 5 (to P. Agostino, Sept. 4, 1915), Advent 6 (to P. Agostino, June 20, 1915), Advent 6 blessing (to P. Benedetto, Dec. 19, 1914), Advent 7 (to P. Benedetto, May 27, 1915), Advent 8 (to P. Benedetto, Dec. 4, 1916), Advent 12 (to P. Agostino, July 1, 1915), Advent 13 blessing (to P. Agostino, Aug. 25, 1915), Advent 15 (to P. Benedetto, Jan. 30, 1921), Advent 17 blessing (to P. Benedetto, Dec. 18, 1920), Advent 18 blessing (to P. Agostino, Dec. 15, 1917), Advent 21 (to P. Benedetto, Nov. 20, 1921), Advent 23 (to P. Benedetto, Mar. 8, 1916), Advent 24 blessing (to P. Benedetto, Dec. 20, 1918), Advent 26 (to P. Agostino, Nov. 19, 1916), Advent 27 (to P. Agostino, Mar. 17, 1916 and Aug. 15, 1916), Advent 28 blessing (to P. Benedetto, Dec. 24, 1921), Christmas 1 (to P. Benedetto, Jan. 29, 1919), Christmas 1 blessing (to P. Agostino, Dec. 28, 1917), Christmas 2 blessing (to P. Benedetto, Jan. 1, 1921), Christmas 3 (to P. Benedetto, Mar. 8, 1916), Christmas 6 (to P. Agostino, July 10, 1915), Christmas 11 (to P. Agostino, Apr. 18, 1912), Christmas 12 blessing (to P. Benedetto, Oct. 8, 1920), and final blessing 3 (to P. Agostino, May 8, 1919).

The following passages from Padre Pio's letters are reprinted from *Padre Pio of Pietrelcina Letters,* volume 2: Correspondence with Raffaelina Cerase, noblewoman, 1914–1915. Ed. by Melchiorre of Pobladura and Alessandro of Ripabottoni, English version ed. by Gerardo Di Flumeri, O.F.M. Cap. San Giovanni Rotondo, Italy: Our Lady of Grace Capuchin Friary, 1997: Advent 3 blessing (June 8, 1915), Advent 11 (Oct. 10, 1914), Advent 11 blessing (Oct. 23, 1914), Advent 14 (Apr. 20, 1915), Advent 17 (Apr. 25, 1914), Advent 22 (Apr. 20, 1915), Christmas 3 blessing (July 14, 1915), and Christmas 7 (Sept. 7, 1915).

The following passages from Padre Pio's letters are reprinted from *Padre Pio of Pietrelcina Letters,* volume 3: Correspondence with his spiritual daughters, 1915–1923. Ed. by Melchiorre of Pobladura and Alessandro of Ripabottoni, English version ed. by Gerardo Di Flumeri, O.F.M. Cap., and Alessio Parente, O.F.M. Cap. San Giovanni Rotondo, Italy: Our Lady of Grace Capuchin Friary, 1994: first epigraph (to Ventrella Sisters, Mar. 8, 1918), Advent 1 blessing (to Vittorina Ventrella, Feb. 12, 1922), Advent 2 blessing (to Maria Gargani, Dec. 27, 1917), Advent 5 blessing (to M. Gargani, Jan. 17, 1919), Advent 8 blessing (to M. Gargani, Apr. 28, 1919), Advent 9 (to Annita Rodote, Oct. 31, 1915), Advent 9 blessing (to unidentified person, June 3, 1917), Advent 10 (to Erminia Gargani, June 28, 1918), Advent 10 blessing (to E. Gargani, Oct. 25, 1919), Advent 13 (to A. Rodote, Aug. 16, 1918), Advent 14 blessing (to Margherita Tresca, Dec. 24, 1917), Advent 15 blessing (to A. Rodote, Mar. 8, 1915), Advent 16 (to A. Rodote, Feb. 6, 1915), Advent 16 blessing (to Lucia Fiorentino, Oct. 27, 1916), Advent 18 (to M. Gargani, Apr. 28, 1919), Advent 19 (to A. Rodote, Aug. 27, 1915), Advent 19 blessing (to V. Ventrella, Nov. 14, 1920), Advent 20 (to M. Gargani, Nov. 4, 1916), Advent 20 blessing (to M. Gargani, Nov. 22, 1916), Advent 21 blessing (to Frieda Folger, Dec. 21, 1922), Advent 22 blessing (to M. Gargani, Nov. 10, 1919), Advent 23 blessing (to Assunta di Tomaso, Jan. 1, 1919), Advent 24 (to the Ventrella Sisters, Dec. 15, 1916), Advent 25 (to E. Gargani, Mar. 3, 1917), Advent 25 blessing (to the Campanile Sisters, Dec. 21, 1918), Advent 26 blessing (to Antonietta Vona, Mar. 29, 1919), Advent 27 blessing (to A. Vona, Aug. 18, 1918), Advent 28 (to E. Gargani, Apr. 11, 1918), Christmas 2 (to the Ventrella Sisters, Oct. 1, 1917), Christmas 4 (to M. Gargani, Nov. 29, 1917), Christmas 4 blessing (to M. Gargani, Dec. 13, 1918), Christmas 5 (to Girolama Longo, July 29, 1920), Christmas 5 blessing (to E. Gargani, Dec. 31, 1922), Christmas 6 blessing (to L. Fiorentino, Jan., 1918), Christmas 7 blessing (to E. Gargani, Dec. 14, 1916), Christmas 8 blessing (to M. Gargani, Dec. 29, 1919), Christmas 9 (to M. Gargani, Dec. 30, 1918), Christmas 9 blessing (to M. Gargani, Dec. 31, 1922), Christmas 10 blessing (to E. Gargani, Dec. 21, 1921), Christmas 11 blessing (to A. Rodote, Oct. 31, 1915), and final blessing 1 (to M. Gargani, Oct. 4, 1917).

The following passages are from "Time of Birth" by Padre Pio, edited by Ezechia Cardone, San Giovanni Rotondo, 1958, as found in the Archives of Padre Pio in San Giovanni Rotondo: Advent 4 blessing (p. 17), Christmas 8 (p. 10), Christmas 10 (p. 41), Christmas 12 (p. 43), final blessing 2 (p. 36).

Advent 3 from "The Five Popes of Padre Pio" by Felice Spaccucci, Naples 1968, p. 32, as found in the Archives of Padre Pio in San Giovanni Rotondo.

Advent 7 blessing from "San Giovanni Rotondo: In the Light of Franciscanism" by Francesco Morcaldi, Parma 1961, pp. 165, 167, as found in the Archives of Padre Pio in San Giovanni Rotondo.

Advent 12 blessing from Padre Pio, *Meditation Prayer on Mary Immaculate,* translation and sketch by Laura Chanler White. Rockford, Ill.: TAN Books and Publishers, 1974.